Brunches

The Family Circle® Promise of Success

Welcome to the world of Confident Cooking, created for you in the
Family Circle® Test Kitchen, where recipes are double-tested by our team
of home economists to achieve a high standard of success.

MURDOCH
B O O K S

pancakes with berry sauce

PREP TIME: 10 MINUTES +
  20 MINUTES STANDING
COOKING TIME: 25 MINUTES
SERVES 4

Berry sauce

60 g (1/4 cup) sugar
2 teaspoons lemon juice
250 g (1 punnet) raspberries

185 g (1 1/2 cups) self-raising flour
1 teaspoon baking powder
2 tablespoons caster (superfine) sugar
pinch of salt
2 eggs, lightly beaten
250 ml (1 cup) milk
60 g (2 oz) butter, melted
raspberries, to serve

NUTRITION PER SERVE: Fat 6 g; Carbohydrate 63 g;
Protein 10.5 g; Dietary Fibre 5 g; Cholesterol 102 mg;
1450 kJ (345 Cal)

1 To make the berry sauce, put the sugar, lemon juice and 3 tablespoons water in a saucepan and bring to the boil over medium heat. Add the raspberries and cook over low heat for 3 minutes. Cool. For a smooth sauce, purée in a food processor for 10 seconds; for a chunky sauce gently mash with a fork until you reach the desired texture.

2 Sift the flour, baking powder, sugar and salt into a bowl and make a well in the centre. Mix together the eggs, milk and butter in a jug and pour into the well all at once, whisking to form a smooth batter. Cover the bowl with plastic wrap and set the batter aside for 20 minutes.

3 Heat a frying pan and brush lightly with melted butter or oil. Pour 3 tablespoons batter into the pan and swirl gently to create a pancake about 10 cm (4 inches) in diameter. Cook over low heat for 1 minute, or until the underside is golden.

4 Turn the pancake over and cook the other side very quickly, for about 10 seconds. Transfer to a plate and keep warm while cooking the remaining batter. Serve stacks of the the pancakes with the berry sauce.

creamed rice with minted citrus compote

PREP TIME: 15 MINUTES
COOKING TIME: 30 MINUTES
SERVES 4

150 g ($^3/_4$ cup) basmati rice
500 ml (2 cups) milk
4 cardamom pods, bruised
$^1/_2$ cinnamon stick
1 clove
3 tablespoons honey
1 teaspoon vanilla essence

Citrus compote
2 ruby grapefruit, peeled and segmented
2 oranges, peeled and segmented
3 tablespoons orange juice
1 teaspoon grated lime zest
3 tablespoons honey
8 mint leaves, finely chopped

NUTRITION PER SERVE: Fat 2.5 g; Carbohydrate 81 g; Protein 9 g; Dietary Fibre 3 g; Cholesterol 9 mg; 1575 kJ (375 Cal)

1 Cook the rice in a large saucepan of boiling water for 12 minutes, stirring occasionally. Drain and cool.

2 Put the rice, milk, cardamom pods, cinnamon stick and clove in a saucepan and bring to the boil. Reduce the heat to low and simmer for 15 minutes, stirring occasionally, until the milk is absorbed and the rice is creamy. Remove the spices, then stir in the honey and vanilla.

3 To make the compote, combine the ruby grapefruit, orange, orange juice, lime zest, honey and mint and mix until the honey has dissolved. Serve with the rice.

variation Here's another compote you could try. Peel 6 apricots and 6 peaches and cut into slices. Dissolve 175 g (6 oz) sugar in 500 ml (2 cups) water and boil for 1 minute. Add the fruit, 24 pitted cherries and the zest of an orange, cut into strips. Simmer for about 2–3 minutes, or until the fruit is tender. Remove the fruit and simmer the syrup until it thickens. Add 4 tablespoons dessert wine if you like. Return the fruit to the pan to warm.

poached eggs with spinach and yoghurt dressing

PREP TIME: 10 MINUTES
COOKING TIME: 15 MINUTES
SERVES 4

125 g ($^1/_2$ cup) sheep's milk yoghurt
1 small garlic clove, crushed
1 tablespoon snipped chives
300 g ($10^1/_2$ oz) baby English spinach
    leaves, washed
30 g (1 oz) butter, chopped
herbed salt
4 tomatoes, halved
1 tablespoon white vinegar
8 eggs
1 round loaf light rye bread, cut into eight
    thick slices

NUTRITION PER SERVE: Fat 20 g; Carbohydrate 45 g;
Protein 25 g; Dietary Fibre 7.5 g; Cholesterol 384 mg;
1895 kJ (453 Cal)

1 To make the dressing, mix together the yoghurt, garlic and chives.

2 Wash the spinach and put it in a large saucepan with a little water clinging to the leaves. Cook, covered, over low heat for 3–4 minutes, or until wilted. Add the butter and season with herbed salt. Set aside and keep warm. Cook the tomatoes under a hot grill (broiler) for 3–5 minutes.

3 Fill a frying pan three-quarters full with cold water and add the vinegar and some salt to stop the egg whites spreading. Bring to a gentle simmer. Gently break one egg into a small bowl and carefully slide it into the water. Repeat with the remaining eggs, then reduce the heat so that the water barely moves. Cook for 1–2 minutes, or until the eggs are just set. Remove with an egg flip. Drain.

4 Toast the bread. Top each slice of toast with spinach, an egg and some dressing. Serve with tomato halves.

variation To make Eggs benedict, serve the eggs on English muffins, with some crispy bacon and hollandaise. To make hollandaise put 2 egg yolks in a blender. Melt 90 g ($3^1/_4$ oz) butter with 1 tablespoon lemon juice until boiling. Switch on the blender and pour the butter through the top onto the yolks: the mixture will thicken as the hot liquid cooks the yolks. Whisk the egg whites until soft peaks form and fold them into the sauce.

power porridge

PREP TIME: 10 MINUTES
COOKING TIME: 20 MINUTES
SERVES 4

400 g (4 cups) rolled oats
105 g (1 cup) rice flakes
130 g (1 cup) barley flakes
130 g (1 cup) rye flakes
205 g (1 cup) millet
2 tablespoons sesame seeds, toasted
2 teaspoons linseed (flax)

NUTRITION PER SERVE: Fat 16 g; Carbohydrate 127 g; Protein 22 g; Dietary Fibre 14.5 g; Cholesterol 0 mg; 3115 kJ (745 Cal)

1 Put the rolled oats, rice flakes, barley flakes, rye flakes, millet, sesame seeds and linseed in a large bowl and stir well. Store in a sealed container until ready to use.

2 To prepare the porridge for four people, put 280 g (2 cups) of the dry mixture, a pinch of salt and 500 ml (2 cups) water in a saucepan, then stir well. Leave for 5 minutes (this creates a smoother, creamier porridge). Stir and add another 500 ml (2 cups) water. Bring to the boil over medium heat, stirring occasionally.

3 Reduce the heat to low and simmer the porridge, stirring frequently, for 12–15 minutes, or until the mixture is soft and creamy and the grains are cooked. Delicious served with milk or low-fat yoghurt and a sprinkling of soft brown sugar.

puffed corn cereal

PREP TIME: 10 MINUTES
COOKING TIME: 15 MINUTES
SERVES 20 (MAKES APPROX. 1.5 KG)

85 g (3 oz) puffed corn
85 g (3 oz) puffed millet
400 g (14 oz) dried fruit and nut mix
175 g (2^1/$_3$ cups) unprocessed natural bran
55 g (1 cup) flaked coconut
60 g (^{1}/$_3$ cup) pepitas
185 ml (^{3}/$_4$ cup) maple syrup
70 g (1 cup) processed bran cereal
400 g (14 oz) dried fruit salad mix, cut into small pieces

NUTRITION PER SERVE: Fat 4 g; Carbohydrate 47 g; Protein 5 g; Dietary Fibre 9 g; Cholesterol 0 mg; 965 kJ (231 Cal)

1 Preheat the oven to 180°C (350°F/ Gas 4). Spread out the corn, millet, fruit and nut mix, bran, coconut and pepitas in a large roasting tin.

2 Pour the maple syrup over the puffed corn mixture and stir thoroughly until well coated.

3 Stir in the bran cereal and fruit salad mix and bake for 15 minutes, or until golden, turning the cereal several times. Cool completely.

lemon grass and ginger infused fruit salad

PREP TIME: 20 MINUTES
COOKING TIME: 10 MINUTES
SERVES 4

60 g (1/4 cup) caster (superfine) sugar
2 x 2 cm (3/4 x 3/4 inch) piece fresh ginger, thinly sliced
1 stem lemon grass, bruised and halved
1 large passionfruit
1 Fiji red papaya (see Notes)
1/2 honeydew melon
1 large mango
1 small fresh pineapple
12 fresh lychees (see Notes)
3 tablespoons mint, shredded

NUTRITION PER SERVE: Fat 2 g; Carbohydrate 80 g; Protein 7 g; Dietary Fibre 13.5 g; Cholesterol 0 mg; 1485 kJ (355 Cal)

1 Put the sugar, ginger and lemon grass in a small saucepan, add 125 ml (1/2 cup) water and stir over low heat to dissolve the sugar. Boil for 5 minutes, or until reduced to 80 ml (1/3 cup) and cool. Strain the syrup and add the passionfruit pulp.

2 Peel and seed the papaya and melon. Cut into 4 cm (1 1/2 inch) cubes. Peel the mango and cut the flesh into cubes, discarding the stone. Peel, halve and core the pineapple and cut into cubes. Peel the lychees, then make a slit in the flesh and carefully remove the seed.

3 Put all the fruit in a large serving bowl. Pour on the syrup, or serve separately if preferred. Garnish with the shredded mint.

notes Papaya is sometimes sold as pawpaw, but is actually a different fruit. The Fiji red papaya is shaped like a football and has reddish flesh.

If fresh lychees are not available, tinned ones are fine.

crepes with warm fruit compote

PREP TIME: 30 MINUTES +
  30 MINUTES STANDING
COOKING TIME: 20 MINUTES
SERVES 4

Crepes

60 g ($^1/_2$ cup) plain (all-purpose) flour
2 eggs
250 ml (1 cup) skim milk
oil spray
2 teaspoons caster (superfine) sugar

Compote

100 g ($3^1/_2$ oz) whole dried apricots
3 tablespoons port or Muscat
1 vanilla bean, halved
2 firm pears, peeled, cored and quartered
2 cinnamon sticks
425 g (15 oz) tin pitted prunes in syrup,
  drained, syrup reserved

NUTRITION PER SERVE: Fat 4 g; Carbohydrate 59 g; Protein 9 g; Dietary Fibre 6 g; Cholesterol 92 mg; 1340 kJ (320 Cal)

1 Sift the flour into a bowl and gradually add the combined eggs and milk, whisking to remove any lumps. Cover the batter with plastic wrap and leave for 30 minutes.

2 Meanwhile, put the apricots and port in a saucepan and cook, covered, over low heat for 2–3 minutes, or until softened. Scrape the seeds from the vanilla bean and add to the pan with the pod, pear, cinnamon and prune syrup. Cover and simmer, stirring occasionally, for 4 minutes, or until the pear has softened. Add the prunes and simmer for I minute.

3 Heat a 20 cm (8 inch) non-stick crepe pan or frying pan over medium heat. Lightly spray with oil. Pour 3 tablespoons batter into the pan and swirl evenly over the base. Cook each crepe for I minute, or until the underside is golden. Turn it over and cook the other side for 30 seconds, and remove. Keep warm and repeat to make eight crepes.

4 Fold the crepes into triangles and sprinkle with caster sugar. Serve with the compote.

apricot and raisin bran loaf

PREP TIME: 15 MINUTES +
   30 MINUTES SOAKING
COOKING TIME: 50 MINUTES
SERVES 6-8

150 g (5¹/2 oz) dried apricots, chopped
160 g (1 cup) raisins
70 g (1 cup) processed bran cereal
95 g (¹/2 cup) lightly packed soft brown
   sugar
375 ml (1¹/2 cups) warm milk
125 g (1 cup) self-raising flour
75 g (¹/2 cup) wholemeal self-raising flour
1 teaspoon mixed spice
icing (confectioners') sugar (optional)

NUTRITION PER SERVE (8): Fat 3 g; Carbohydrate 52.5 g; Protein 6.5 g; Dietary Fibre 7 g; Cholesterol 6.5 mg; 1085 kJ (260 Cal)

1 Preheat the oven to 180°C (350°F/ Gas 4). Grease a deep 18 x 11 cm (7 x 4¹/2 inch) loaf tin and line the base and sides with baking paper.

2 Soak the apricots, raisins, bran cereal and brown sugar in the milk in a large bowl for 30 minutes, or until the milk is almost completely absorbed. Sift in the flours and mixed spice, then stir to form a stiff, moist batter.

3 Spoon the mixture into the prepared tin and smooth the surface. Bake for 50 minutes, or until a skewer comes out clean when inserted into the centre of the cake; cover with foil during cooking if it browns too much. Leave in the tin for 10 minutes before turning out onto a wire rack to cool. Cut into thick slices. Dust with icing sugar and serve with butter.

note Use any dried fruit combination. This loaf is delicious toasted.

waffles and maple syrup with ricotta

PREP TIME: 15 MINUTES + 1 HOUR STANDING
COOKING TIME: 20 MINUTES
SERVES 6

200 g (7 oz) plain (all-purpose) flour
1 1/2 tablespoons caster (superfine) sugar
1 tablespoon baking powder
50 g (1 3/4 oz) rolled oats
1 egg yolk
350 ml (1 1/3 cups) milk
2 teaspoons butter, melted
3 egg whites
100 g (3 1/2 oz) ricotta cheese
2 tablespoons vanilla yoghurt
3 tablespoons maple syrup, plus extra

NUTRITION PER SERVE: Fat 7 g; Carbohydrate 47 g;
Protein 11 g; Dietary Fibre 2 g; Cholesterol 48 mg;
1220 kJ (290 Cal)

1 Sift the flour, sugar, baking powder and 1/2 teaspoon salt into a bowl, then stir in the oats. Add the combined egg yolk and milk with the butter and mix.

2 Whisk the egg whites in a clean, dry bowl until soft peaks form, then gently fold into the batter with a metal spoon. Cover and leave for 1 hour. Beat together the ricotta, yoghurt and maple syrup until smooth.

3 Preheat a waffle maker. Pour a sixth of the mixture into the waffle maker and cook for 2–3 minutes. Repeat with the rest of the mixture to make six waffles. To serve, put each waffle on a plate, top with some ricotta mixture and drizzle with the extra maple syrup.

french toast

PREP TIME: 5 MINUTES
COOKING TIME: 10 MINUTES
SERVES 2

1 tablespoon cream
2 eggs
2 tablespoons caster (superfine) sugar
6 slices bread (either fresh or day-old bread is suitable)
25 g (1 oz) butter

NUTRITION PER SERVE: Fat 22 g; Carbohydrate 61 g;
Protein 14.5 g; Dietary Fibre 3 g; Cholesterol 231 mg;
2045 kJ (490 Cal)

1 Mix together the cream, eggs and sugar. Dip the bread, one slice at a time, into the milk and egg mixture, ensuring both sides are soaked.

2 Heat a knob of butter in a frying pan. Remove the bread from the mixture, drain off the excess liquid and cook on both sides until golden brown and cooked through—you will probably need to do this in batches. Serve sprinkled with cinnamon and sugar or drizzle with maple syrup.

low-fat banana bread with maple ricotta and fresh fruit

PREP TIME: 10 MINUTES
COOKING TIME: 55 MINUTES
MAKES 10-12 SLICES

4 tablespoons strong coffee
125 g ($^2/_3$ cup) soft brown sugar
1 egg
1 egg white
3 tablespoons vegetable oil
1 teaspoon vanilla essence
3 ripe bananas, mashed (about 1$^1/_4$ cups)
125 g (1 cup) plain (all-purpose) flour
250 g (2 cups) self-raising flour
$^1/_2$ teaspoon baking powder
1 teaspoon ground ginger
$^1/_2$ teaspoon ground nutmeg
1 teaspoon ground cinnamon
1 teaspoon bicarbonate of soda
fresh fruit (strawberries, banana, kiwi fruit,
    berries), to serve

Maple ricotta
200 g (7 oz) low-fat ricotta cheese
2 tablespoons maple syrup

NUTRITION PER SLICE (12): Fat 7 g; Carbohydrate 45 g;
Protein 8 g; Dietary Fibre 3.5 g; Cholesterol 22.6 mg;
1135 kJ (270 Cal)

1 Preheat the oven to 170°C (325°F/ Gas 3). Lightly grease a 22 x 12 cm (9 x 4$^1/_2$ inch) loaf tin and line the base with baking paper. Heat the coffee in a small saucepan over low heat, add the soft brown sugar and stir until the sugar has dissolved.

2 Place the egg, egg white, oil and vanilla essence in a bowl and beat together until just combined. Add the sweetened strong coffee and the mashed banana.

3 Sift the plain and self-raising flours, baking powder, ginger, nutmeg, cinnamon and bicarbonate of soda onto the mixture and stir gently to combine—do not overbeat. Spoon the mixture into the prepared loaf tin.

4 Bake for 50 minutes, or until a skewer comes out clean when inserted into the centre. Leave in the tin for 10 minutes before turning out onto a wire rack to cool completely.

5 To make the maple ricotta, place the ricotta and maple syrup in a small bowl and mix until well combined. Cut the banana bread into thick slices and serve with the maple ricotta and fresh fruit. Also delicious toasted.

stone fruits with cinnamon toast

PREP TIME: 10 MINUTES
COOKING TIME: 10 MINUTES
SERVES 4

2 tablespoons butter
1 1/2 teaspoons ground cinnamon
4 thick slices good-quality brioche
4 ripe plums, halved and stones removed
4 ripe nectarines, halved and stones removed
2 tablespoons honey, warmed

NUTRITION PER SERVE: Fat 13 g; Carbohydrate 66 g; Protein 9 g; Dietary Fibre 7 g; Cholesterol 41 mg; 1730 kJ (415 Cal)

1 Put the butter and 1 teaspoon of the ground cinnamon in a bowl and mix until well combined. Grill the brioche on one side until golden. Spread the other side with half the cinnamon spread, then grill until golden. Keep warm in the oven.

2 Brush the fruit with the remaining spread and cook under a grill (broiler) or on a chargrill pan or barbecue hot plate, until the spread is bubbling and the fruit is tinged at the edges.

3 To serve, put two plum halves and two nectarine halves on each toasted slice of brioche. Dust with the remaining cinnamon and drizzle with the warmed honey. Dollop with a little fromage frais, if desired.

note Tinned plums or apricots may be used in place of fresh stone fruits.

peachy keen smoothie

PREP TIME: 15 MINUTES
COOKING TIME: NIL
SERVES 2

185 g (3/4 cup) low-fat peach and mango yoghurt
185 ml (3/4 cup) apricot nectar, chilled
60 g (1/2 cup) raspberries
300 g (1 1/2 cups) ripe diced peaches
8 large ice cubes
peach wedges, to serve

NUTRITION PER SERVE: Fat 0.5 g; Carbohydrate 35 g; Protein 7 g; Dietary Fibre 3.5 g; Cholesterol 3 g; 770 kJ (185 Cal)

1 Put the yoghurt, nectar, fruit and ice in a blender and blend until smooth.

2 Pour into two glasses and serve with the peach wedges.

pictured: stone fruits with cinnamon toast

healthy fruit muffins

PREP TIME: 15 MINUTES +
   5 MINUTES SOAKING
COOKING TIME: 20 MINUTES
MAKES 12

160 g (1 cup) chopped mixed dried fruits
225 g (1½ cups) wholemeal self-raising flour
1 teaspoon baking powder
150 g (1 cup) unprocessed oat bran
60 g (⅓ cup) soft brown sugar
290 ml (10 fl oz) skim milk
1 egg
1 tablespoon oil

NUTRITION PER MUFFIN: Fat 3.5 g; Carbohydrate 33 g;
Protein 6 g; Dietary Fibre 4.5 g; Cholesterol 16.5 mg;
755 kJ (180 Cal)

1 Preheat the oven to 180°C (350°F/ Gas 4). Grease twelve 125 ml (½ cup) muffin holes. Soak the dried fruit in a bowl with 3 tablespoons boiling water for 5 minutes.

2 Sift the flour and baking powder into a large bowl, returning the husks to the bowl. Stir in the oat bran and sugar and make a well in the centre.

3 Combine the milk, egg and oil in a jug. Add the soaked fruit and milk mixture all at once to the dry ingredients. Fold in gently using a metal spoon, until just combined.

4 Divide evenly among the muffin holes. Bake for 20 minutes, or until golden and a skewer inserted into the centre comes out clean. Cool for a few minutes in the tin, then turn out onto a wire rack.

pineapple and coconut iced drink

PREP TIME: 10 MINUTES +
   FREEZING + CHILLING TIME
COOKING TIME: NIL
SERVES 2

500 ml (2 cups) fresh pineapple juice
250 ml (1 cup) coconut milk
mint leaves, to garnish
pineapple leaves, to garnish

NUTRITION PER SERVE: Fat 25 g; Carbohydrate 30 g;
Protein 3.5 g; Dietary Fibre 6 g; Cholesterol 0 g;
1520 kJ (365 cal)

1 Combine the pineapple juice with the coconut milk in a large jug and mix well. Pour 125 ml (½ cup) of the mixture into eight holes of an ice cube tray and freeze. Chill the remaining mixture in the refrigerator.

2 When the the ice cubes have frozen, pour the chilled juice mixture into two glasses, add the frozen cubes and garnish with the mint and pineapple leaves.

pictured: healthy fruit muffins

egg and bacon pie

PREP TIME: 20 MINUTES + 30 MINUTES
   REFRIGERATION + COOLING
COOKING TIME: 50 MINUTES
SERVES 4-6

Pastry

450 g (1 lb) plain (all-purpose) flour
125 g (4^1/$_2$ oz) butter, chilled and cubed
250 g (9 oz) mascarpone

1 tablespoon olive oil
300 g (10^1/$_2$ oz) bacon, diced
2 onions, halved and thinly sliced
1 tablespoon chopped flat-leaf (Italian)
   parsley
6 eggs
1 egg yolk

NUTRITION PER SERVE (6): Fat 43.5 g; Carbohydrate 59 g;
Protein 29.5 g; Dietary Fibre 3.5 g; Cholesterol 332 mg;
3085 kJ (735 Cal)

1 Sift the flour into a bowl and rub in the butter with your fingertips until the mixture resembles fine breadcrumbs. Add the mascarpone and mix with a flat-bladed knife, using a cutting action, until the mixture begins to form lumps which leave the side of the bowl.

2 Turn the dough out onto a lightly floured surface and gently gather into a smooth ball. Flatten slightly into a disc, then cover in plastic wrap and refrigerate for 30 minutes.

3 Preheat the oven to 170°C (325°F/ Gas 3). Lightly grease a 23 cm (9 inch) metal pie dish. Put a baking tray in the oven to preheat. Heat the oil in a frying pan and cook the bacon and onion over medium heat, stirring occasionally, for 5–7 minutes, or until just browning. Stir in the parsley. Set aside to cool.

4 Divide the pastry into two portions, one slightly larger than the other. Roll out the larger portion between two sheets of baking paper until large enough to line the base and side of the pie dish. Line the pie dish. Put the bacon mixture in the pastry shell and make six well-spaced holes in the mixture with the back of a spoon. Crack an egg into each of the holes. Brush the rim of the pastry with water. Roll out the remaining pastry between the baking paper until large enough to cover the top of the pie. Lift it onto the pie, trim the excess pastry and seal the edges. Re-roll the trimmings and make leaves to decorate the pie. Brush with egg yolk and bake on the hot tray for 40 minutes; cover if it browns too quickly. Leave for 10 minutes, then serve.

omelette with asparagus, smoked salmon and dill

PREP TIME: 10 MINUTES
COOKING TIME: 10 MINUTES
SERVES 2

6 egg whites
6 eggs
2 tablespoons low-fat ricotta cheese
2 tablespoons chopped dill
425 g (15 oz) fresh asparagus, cut into
    5 cm lengths
100 g (3¹/2 oz) smoked salmon, thinly sliced
lemon wedges, to garnish
sprigs of dill, to garnish

NUTRITION PER SERVE: Fat 19 g; Carbohydrate 4 g; Protein 49 g; Dietary Fibre 3 g; Cholesterol 595 mg; 1620 kJ (390 Cal)

1 Whisk the egg whites until foaming. In a separate bowl, whisk the whole eggs and ricotta until combined. Add the whites. Season and stir in the dill.

2 Bring a saucepan of lightly salted water to the boil. Add the asparagus and cook for 1–2 minutes, or until tender but still firm to the bite. Drain and refresh in iced water.

3 Heat a non-stick 23 cm (9 inch) frying pan over low heat and spray lightly with oil spray. Pour in half the egg mixture and arrange half the asparagus on top. Cook over medium heat until the egg is just setting. Flip one side onto the other and transfer to a serving plate. Repeat with the remaining mixture. Top the omelettes with smoked salmon, and garnish with lemon wedges and a sprig of dill.

smoked salmon, camembert and dill frittata

PREP TIME: 20 MINUTES
COOKING TIME: 50 MINUTES
SERVES 6-8

12 eggs
¹/2 cup (50 g) grated Parmesan cheese
600 ml (2¹/2 cups) cream
6 spring onions (scallions), sliced
200 g (7 oz) smoked salmon
3 tablespoons chopped dill
100 g (3¹/2 oz) Camembert cheese, sliced
1 teaspoon lemon zest, to garnish

NUTRITION PER SERVE (8): Fat 45 g; Protein 20 g; Carbohydrate 3 g; Dietary Fibre 0 g; Cholesterol 407 mg; 2110 kJ (505 Cal)

1 Preheat the oven to 180°C (350°F/ Gas 4). Lightly grease a 23 cm (9 inch) springform cake tin and line the base with baking paper.

2 Lightly beat the eggs, Parmesan, cream and spring onion together. Thinly slice 150 g (5¹/2 oz) of the smoked salmon and add it and the dill to the egg mixture. Pour into the tin and place on a baking tray. Bake for about 50 minutes, or until set.

3 Cool slightly before removing from the tin. Arrange the Camembert and remaining salmon in the centre, then garnish with lemon zest. Serve warm.

pictured: omelette with asparagus, smoked salmon and dill

baked ricotta and red capsicum with pesto

PREP TIME: 10 MINUTES
COOKING TIME: 45 MINUTES
SERVES 6

1 large red capsicum (pepper), cut into
    quarters and seeded
750 g (1 lb 10 oz) low-fat ricotta cheese
1 egg
6 slices wholegrain bread

Pesto

2 tablespoons pine nuts
100 g (2 cups) basil
2 garlic cloves
2 tablespoons good-quality olive oil
2 tablespoons finely grated fresh
    Parmesan cheese

NUTRITION PER SERVE: Fat 21 g; Carbohydrate 22 g;
Protein 20 g; Dietary Fibre 2.5 g; Cholesterol 72 mg;
1530 kJ (365 Cal)

1 Preheat the oven to 180°C (350°F/ Gas 4). Lightly grease six Texas (large) muffin holes.

2 Cook the capsicum, skin-side up, under a hot grill (broiler) for 5–6 minutes, or until the skin blackens and blisters. Place in a bowl and cover with plastic wrap until cool enough to handle. Peel off the skin and slice the flesh into 2 cm (³/₄ inch) wide strips.

3 To make the pesto, place the pine nuts, basil and garlic in a food processor and process for 15 seconds, or until finely chopped. While the processor is running add the oil in a continuous thin stream, then season with salt and freshly ground black pepper. Stir in the Parmesan.

4 Mix the ricotta and egg until well combined. Season with salt and freshly ground black pepper. Divide the capsicum strips among the muffin holes, top with 2 teaspoons pesto and spoon in the ricotta mixture.

5 Bake for 35–40 minutes, or until the ricotta is firm and golden. Cool, then remove from the muffin holes. Toast the bread slices and cut them into fingers. Serve with the baked ricotta and a dollop of the remaining pesto on the side.

eggs en cocotte

PREP TIME: 15 MINUTES
COOKING TIME: 30 MINUTES
SERVES 4

Tomato sauce
1 tablespoon olive oil
1 garlic clove, crushed
3 vine-ripened tomatoes, peeled, seeded
   and chopped

1/2 teaspoon olive oil
4 eggs
Tabasco sauce, to taste
2 tablespoons chives, snipped with
   scissors
4 thick slices multigrain bread
butter, to serve

NUTRITION PER SERVE: Fat 15 g; Carbohydrate 20 g;
Protein 11 g; Dietary Fibre 3 g; Cholesterol 187.5 mg;
1075 kJ (255 Cal)

1 Preheat the oven to 180°C (350°F/ Gas 4). To make the sauce, heat the oil in a heavy-based frying pan. Add the garlic and cook for 1 minute, or until it begins to turn golden. Add the tomato and season with salt and pepper. Cook over medium heat for 15 minutes, or until thickened.

2 Lightly grease four 125 ml (1/2 cup) ramekins with the olive oil, then carefully break 1 egg into each, trying not to break the yolk. Pour the tomato sauce evenly around the outside of each egg so the yolk is still visible. Add a little Tabasco sauce, then sprinkle with chives and season lightly with salt and freshly ground black pepper.

3 Put the ramekins in a deep baking tray and pour in enough hot water to come halfway up the side of the ramekins. Bake for 10–12 minutes, or until the egg white is set. Toast and lightly butter the bread, then cut into thick fingers. Serve with the egg.

cheese and onion waffles with herbed ricotta and roast tomato

PREP TIME: 20 MINUTES
COOKING TIME: 1 HOUR 15 MINUTES
SERVES 4

4 Roma (plum) tomatoes, cut in half
1 tablespoon olive oil
1 tablespoon balsamic vinegar
1 teaspoon sugar
1 tablespoon chopped oregano
310 g (1¼ cups) low-fat ricotta cheese
4 tablespoons chopped herbs (oregano,
    sage, rosemary, parsley)
185 g (1½ cups) self-raising flour
3 tablespoons freshly grated Parmesan
    cheese
3 tablespoons grated low-fat Cheddar
    cheese
3 large spring onions (scallions),
    finely chopped
1 egg
250 ml (1 cup) low-fat milk
2 egg whites
oregano sprigs, to garnish

NUTRITION PER SERVE: Fat 14 g; Carbohydrate 41 g;
Protein 24 g; Dietary Fibre 3.5 g; Cholesterol 84.5 mg;
1620 kJ (385 Cal)

1 Preheat the oven to 160°C (315°F/ Gas 2–3). Lightly grease an oven tray. Put the tomato halves on the tray and drizzle the cut surface with olive oil and balsamic vinegar. Sprinkle with the sugar, oregano and a little salt. Bake for 1 hour, or until very soft.

2 Put the ricotta in a bowl and fold in the chopped herbs. Season to taste. Using two tablespoons, shape the herbed ricotta into eight long egg shapes. Refrigerate until needed.

3 Meanwhile, sift the flour into a bowl, then add the Parmesan, Cheddar, spring onion, whole egg and milk. Season with salt and freshly ground black pepper, then mix well. Whisk the egg whites until soft peaks form and gently fold into the cheese and egg mixture.

4 Preheat a waffle iron and brush lightly with olive oil. Pour in 4 tablespoons waffle batter and cook until golden on both sides. Keep warm in the oven while you cook the remaining waffles (you should have four in total).

5 To serve, arrange two waffle halves on each serving plate with two tomato halves and two ricotta balls on the side. Garnish with a sprig of oregano.

corn and polenta pancakes with tomato salsa

PREP TIME: 15 MINUTES
COOKING TIME: 10 MINUTES
SERVES 4

Tomato salsa

2 ripe tomatoes
150 g (1 cup) frozen broad (fava) beans
2 tablespoons chopped basil
1 small Lebanese (short) cucumber, diced
2 small garlic cloves, crushed
1 1/2 tablespoons balsamic vinegar
1 tablespoon extra virgin olive oil

Corn and polenta pancakes

90 g (3/4 cup) self-raising flour
110 g (3/4 cup) fine polenta
250 ml (1 cup) milk
300 g (10 1/2 oz) tin corn kernels, drained
olive oil, for pan-frying

NUTRITION PER SERVE: Fat 18.5 g; Carbohydrate 56 g; Protein 11 g; Dietary Fibre 8.5 g; Cholesterol 8.5 mg; 1809 kJ (432 Cal)

1 Score a cross in the base of each tomato, then put in a bowl of boiling water for 30 seconds. Plunge into cold water and peel the skin away from the cross. Dice. Pour boiling water over the broad beans and leave for 2–3 minutes. Drain and rinse under cold water. Remove the skins. Put the beans in a bowl, add the tomato, basil, cucumber, garlic, vinegar and extra virgin olive oil and stir well.

2 To make the pancakes, sift the flour into a bowl and stir in the polenta. Add the milk and corn and stir until just combined, adding more milk if the mixture is too dry. Season.

3 Heat the oil in a large frying pan and spoon half the mixture into the frying pan, making four 9 cm (3 1/2 inch) pancakes. Cook for 2 minutes each side, or until golden and cooked through. Repeat with the remaining mixture, adding more oil if necessary. Drain on crumpled paper towels. Serve with the salsa.

buckwheat blinis
with salmon

PREP TIME: 15 MINUTES +
   45 MINUTES PROVING
COOKING TIME: 20 MINUTES
MAKES 30

7 g ($^1/_8$ oz) sachet dried yeast
pinch of sugar
250 ml (1 cup) milk
40 g ($^1/_3$ cup) plain (all-purpose) flour
100 g ($^3/_4$ cup) buckwheat flour
2 eggs, separated
25 g (1 oz) butter, melted
4 tablespoons oil
300 g (10$^1/_2$ oz) smoked salmon,
   cut into 2 cm ($^3/_4$ inch) strips
50 g (1$^3/_4$ oz) salmon roe
150 ml (5 fl oz) crème fraîche
dill sprigs, to garnish

NUTRITION PER BLINI: Fat 8 g; Carbohydrate 4 g;
Protein 4.5 g; Dietary fibre 0.5 g; Cholesterol 39 mg;
445 kJ (105 Cal)

1 Combine the yeast and sugar in a bowl. Warm the milk over low heat, then gradually stir into the yeast and sugar. Sift the flours and make a well in the centre. Add the egg yolks and warm milk mixture, and whisk until smooth. Cover and leave in a warm place for 45 minutes to prove.

2 Stir in the butter and season. Beat the egg whites with electric beaters until soft peaks form. Fold one-third of the egg whites into the batter until combined, then gently fold in the remaining egg whites.

3 Heat 1 tablespoon of the oil in a frying pan over medium heat. Drop 1 tablespoon of batter per blini into the pan and cook for 1 minute, or until small bubbles form. Turn and cook for 30 seconds, or until golden. Repeat to make 30 blinis. Allow to cool.

4 Using a 6 cm (2$^1/_2$ inch) cutter, trim each blini. Top with a strip of smoked salmon, $^1/_4$ teaspoon of salmon roe and 1 teaspoon of crème fraîche. Season with freshly ground black pepper and garnish with the dill.

mixed mushrooms in brioche

PREP TIME: 15 MINUTES
COOKING TIME: 20 MINUTES
SERVES 6

750 g (1 lb 10 oz) mixed mushrooms
  (Swiss brown, shiitake, button, field,
  oyster)
70 g (2^1/$_2$ oz) butter
4 spring onions (scallions), chopped
2 garlic cloves, crushed
125 ml (^{1}/$_2$ cup) dry white wine
300 ml (9^1/$_2$ fl oz) cream
2 tablespoons chopped thyme
6 small brioche (see Note)

NUTRITION PER SERVE: Fat 33 g; Carbohydrate 15 g;
Protein 7.5 g; Dietary Fibre 4 g; Cholesterol 100 mg;
1587 kJ (380 Cal)

1 Preheat the oven to 180°C (350°F/ Gas 4). Wipe the mushrooms with a clean damp cloth to remove any dirt. Cut the larger mushrooms into thick slices but leave the smaller ones whole.

2 Heat the butter in a large frying pan over medium heat. Add the spring onion and garlic and cook for 2 minutes. Increase the heat, add the mushrooms and cook, stirring frequently, for 5 minutes, or until the mushrooms are soft and all the liquid has evaporated. Pour in the wine and boil for 2 minutes to reduce slightly.

3 Stir in the cream and boil for a further 5 minutes to reduce and slightly thicken the sauce. Season to taste with salt and freshly ground black pepper. Stir in the thyme and set aside for 5 minutes.

4 Slice the top off the brioche and, using your fingers, pull out a quarter of the bread. Put the brioche and their tops on a baking tray and warm in the oven for 5 minutes.

5 Put each brioche onto individual serving plates. Spoon the mushroom sauce into each brioche, allowing it to spill over one side. Replace the top and serve warm.

note Brioche are available from patisseries. You can use bread rolls instead, but the flavour isn't as good.

spinach salad with bacon and quail eggs

PREP TIME: 30 MINUTES
COOKING TIME: 15 MINUTES
SERVES 4-6

12 quail eggs
2 teaspoons oil
4 good-quality streaky bacon rashers,
    cut into thin strips
300 g (10^1/$_2$ oz) baby English spinach
200 g (7 oz) cherry tomatoes, halved
100 g (^{2}/$_3$ cup) pine nuts, toasted

Dressing

3 tablespoons apple cider vinegar
3 garlic cloves, crushed
2 teaspoons Dijon mustard
2 teaspoons maple syrup
1 teaspoon Worcestershire sauce
3 tablespoons olive oil

NUTRITION PER SERVE (6): Fat 27 g; Carbohydrate 4 g; Protein 12 g; Dietary fibre 3 g; Cholesterol 168 mg; 1260 kJ (300 Cal)

1 Bring a small saucepan of water to the boil, gently add the quail eggs and simmer for 1^1/$_2$ minutes. Drain, then refresh under cold running water until cool, then peel the eggs.

2 Heat the oil in a non-stick frying pan over medium heat, add the bacon and cook for 5–6 minutes, or until crisp. Drain on paper towels, retaining the drippings in the pan.

3 Wash the spinach in cold water and remove the stems. Wrap the leaves loosely in a clean tea towel to remove any excess water. Put in a salad bowl, tearing the larger leaves if necessary, then add the tomatoes, bacon and pine nuts. Halve the eggs and scatter over the salad.

4 Reheat the bacon fat over medium heat, then add the vinegar, garlic, mustard, maple syrup and Worcestershire sauce. Shake the pan over the heat, for 2 minutes, or until bubbling, then add the oil and heat for another minute. Pour the warm dressing over the salad, season to taste and serve.

caesar salad

PREP TIME: 20 MINUTES
COOKING TIME: 15 MINUTES
SERVES 4–6

3 eggs
3 garlic cloves, crushed
2–3 anchovy fillets
1 teaspoon Worcestershire sauce
2 tablespoons lime juice
1 teaspoon Dijon mustard
185 ml ($3/4$ cup) olive oil
3 slices white bread
25 g (1 oz) butter
1 tablespoon oil, extra
3 back bacon rashers
1 large or 4 baby cos (romaine) lettuces
75 g ($3/4$ cup) shaved Parmesan cheese

NUTRITION PER SERVE (6): Fat 41 g; Carbohydrate 8 g;
Protein 14 g; Dietary Fibre 1.5 g; Cholesterol 124 mg;
1880 kJ (450 Cal)

1 Process the eggs, garlic, anchovies, Worcestershire sauce, lime juice and mustard in a food processor until smooth. With the motor running, add the oil in a thin, continuous stream to produce a creamy dressing. Season to taste with salt and black pepper.

2 Cut the crusts off the bread, then cut the bread into 1.5 cm ($5/8$ inch) cubes. Heat the butter and extra olive oil in a frying pan over medium heat, add the bread and cook for about 6 minutes, or until crisp, then remove from the pan. Cook the bacon in the same pan for 3 minutes, or until it is crispy and golden, then break into bite-sized pieces.

3 Toss the lettuce leaves with the dressing, then stir in the croutons and bacon, and top with the shaved Parmesan cheese.

roasted tomato and bocconcini salad

PREP TIME: 15 MINUTES
COOKING TIME: 2 HOURS
SERVES 6

8 Roma (plum) tomatoes, halved
pinch of sugar
125 ml ($1/2$ cup) olive oil
3 tablespoons torn basil leaves
2 tablespoons balsamic vinegar
150 g ($5^1/2$ oz) mizuna lettuce
350 g (12 oz) baby bocconcini cheese

NUTRITION PER SERVE: Fat 15 g; Carbohydrate 2 g; Protein 11 g; Dietary Fibre 1.5 g; Cholesterol 20.5 mg; 790 kJ (190 Cal)

1 Preheat the oven to 150°C (300°F/ Gas 2). Put the tomato, cut-side up, on a rack over an oven tray. Sprinkle with salt, black pepper and a pinch of sugar. Roast for 2 hours, then remove from the oven and allow to cool.

2 Combine the oil and basil in a saucepan, and stir gently over medium heat for 3–5 minutes, or until very hot, but not smoking. Remove from the heat and discard the basil. Mix 2 tablespoons of oil with the vinegar. Store the rest in the refrigerator.

3 Toss together the tomato, lettuce and bocconcini. Arrange the salad in a shallow serving bowl and drizzle with the dressing.

note If baby bocconcini are not available, use regular bocconcini and cut them into quarters.

salad pizza

PREP TIME: 15 MINUTES
COOKING TIME: 15 MINUTES
SERVES 4

4 ready-made individual thick pizza bases
2 tablespoons tomato paste (purée)
2 teaspoons chopped oregano
60 g ($2^1/4$ oz) feta cheese, crumbled
100 g ($2/3$ cup) grated mozzarella cheese
65 g ($2/3$ cup) grated Parmesan cheese
100 g ($3^1/2$ oz) baby rocket (arugula) leaves, trimmed
3 tablespoons flat-leaf (Italian) parsley
$1/4$ small red onion, thinly sliced
3 tablespoons olive oil
1 tablespoon lemon juice
1 teaspoon Dijon mustard
50 g ($1^3/4$ oz) Parmesan cheese, extra, shaved

NUTRITION PER SERVE: Fat 30 g; Carbohydrate 25 g; Protein 20 g; Dietary Fibre 4 g; Cholesterol 31 mg; 1866 kJ (445 Cal)

1 Preheat the oven to 200°C (400°F/ Gas 6). Put the pizza bases on baking trays. Spread with tomato paste and sprinkle with oregano, feta and the grated cheeses. Bake for 12 minutes, or until bubbling.

2 Meanwhile, combine the rocket, parsley and onion in a bowl.

3 Whisk together the oil, lemon juice and Dijon mustard, then toss through the salad.

4 Top the pizzas with salad and sprinkle with shaved Parmesan.

pictured: roasted tomato and bocconcini salad

pear and walnut salad with blue cheese dressing

PREP TIME: 20 MINUTES
COOKING TIME: 3 MINUTES
SERVES 4

Dressing
100 g (3¹/₂ oz) creamy blue cheese
3 tablespoons olive oil
1 tablespoon walnut oil
1 tablespoon lemon juice
1 tablespoon cream
2 teaspoons finely chopped sage

100 g (1 cup) walnut halves
4 firm, ripe small pears, such as Corella
2 tablespoons lemon juice
2 witlof (chicory/Belgian endives), trimmed
   and leaves separated
100 g (3¹/₂ oz) Parmesan cheese, shaved

NUTRITION PER SERVE: Fat 53.5 g; Carbohydrate 19 g;
Protein 21 g;Dietary Fibre 7 g; Cholesterol 55.5 mg;
2645 kJ (630 Cal)

1 To make the dressing, purée the blue cheese in a small food processor, then add the olive oil, walnut oil and lemon juice, and blend until smooth. With the motor running, slowly add 2 teaspoons warm water. Stir in the cream and sage, and season to taste.

2 Preheat the grill (broiler). Put the walnuts in a bowl and cover with boiling water. Soak for 1 minute, then drain. Spread the walnuts on a baking tray and put under the grill for 3 minutes, or until lightly toasted. Chop coarsely.

3 Thinly slice across the pears through the core to make rounds. Do not peel or core the pears, but discard the seeds. As each pear is sliced, sprinkle with a little lemon juice to prevent discoloration. On each serving plate, arrange three pear slices in a circle. Top with a scattering of walnuts, a couple of endive leaves, a few more walnuts and some Parmesan shavings. Repeat this layering, reserving the last layer of Parmesan and some of the walnuts. Spoon some dressing over each stack, scatter with the remaining walnuts, and top each with the reserved Parmesan.

avocado, bacon and tomato salad

PREP TIME: 20 MINUTES
COOKING TIME: 35 MINUTES
SERVES 4

6 garlic cloves, unpeeled (see Notes)
4 tablespoons olive oil
1 1/2 tablespoons balsamic vinegar
2 teaspoons Dijon mustard
250 g (9 oz) rindless, smoked back bacon
  (see Notes)
100 g (3 1/2 oz) green salad leaves
1 small red onion, halved and sliced
2 avocados, peeled and cut into
  1.5 cm (5/8 inch) chunks
450 g (1 lb) firm, ripe tomatoes, cut into
  1.5 cm (5/8 inch) chunks

NUTRITION PER SERVE: Fat 43 g; Carbohydrate 4 g; Protein 15 g; Dietary Fibre 4 g; Cholesterol 35.5 mg; 1905 kJ (455 Cal)

1 Preheat the oven to 180°C (350°F/ Gas 4). Put the garlic on a baking tray and roast in the oven for 30 minutes. Allow the garlic to cool, then squeeze out the flesh and mash in a small bowl. Add the olive oil, balsamic vinegar and Dijon mustard, and whisk together well. Season with salt and freshly ground black pepper.

2 Chop the bacon into bite-sized pieces then grill or dry-fry for about 4 minutes, or until it is crispy. Put the salad leaves in a serving bowl and add the bacon, sliced onion, avocado and tomato. Toss together well. Whisk the dressing ingredients again to ensure they are well combined, then pour it over the salad.

notes While this may seem like a lot of garlic, roasting the cloves will give a soft, sweet flavour, which will not overpower the salad.

Smoked back bacon is available from most delicatessens. You can use bacon rashers instead.

vegetable terrine

PREP TIME: 30 MINUTES +
 OVERNIGHT REFRIGERATION
COOKING TIME: NIL
SERVES 8

8 large slices chargrilled eggplant
 (aubergine), drained
10 slices chargrilled red capsicum
 (pepper), drained
8 slices chargrilled zucchini (courgette),
 drained
350 g (12 oz) ricotta cheese
2 garlic cloves, crushed
50 g (1³/4 oz) rocket (arugula) leaves
3 marinated artichokes, drained and sliced
85 g (3 oz) semi-dried (sun-blushed)
 tomatoes, drained and chopped
100 g (3¹/2 oz) marinated mushrooms,
 drained and halved

NUTRITION PER SERVE: Fat 6 g; Carbohydrate 6 g;
Protein 8 g; Dietary Fibre 4 g; Cholesterol 21.5 mg;
440 kJ (105 Cal)

1 Line a 23 x 13 cm (9 x 5 inch) loaf tin with plastic wrap, leaving a generous overhang on each side. Line the base with half the eggplant, cutting to fit. Next layer in half the capsicum, then all of the zucchini.

2 Beat the ricotta cheese and garlic together until smooth. Season with salt and pepper, then spread evenly over the zucchini. Press down firmly, and top with the rocket leaves. Arrange the artichoke, tomato and mushrooms in three strips over the rocket.

3 Top with another layer of capsicum and finish with the eggplant. Cover securely with the overhanging plastic wrap. Top with a piece of cardboard and weigh it down. Chill overnight.

4 Peel back the plastic wrap and carefully turn out the terrine onto a plate. Remove the plastic wrap and cut into thick slices to serve.

chipolatas with cheese and jalapeño quesadillas

PREP TIME: 15 MINUTES
COOKING TIME: 1 HOUR
SERVES 4–6

2 tablespoons olive oil
1 garlic clove, crushed
2 x 400 g (14 oz) tins chopped tomatoes
1/2 teaspoon ground cumin
16 x 15 cm (6 inch) flour tortillas
320 g (11 1/2 oz) coarsely grated Cheddar
  cheese
60 g (1/3 cup) pickled Jalapeño chillies,
  drained and roughly chopped
20 chipolatas
coriander (cilantro) sprigs, to garnish

NUTRITION PER SERVE (6): Fat 48 g; Carbohydrate 34 g;
Protein 31 g; Dietary Fibre 5 g; Cholesterol 115 mg;
2890 kJ (690 Cal)

1 Heat the olive oil in a frying pan over medium heat and cook the garlic for 1–2 minutes, or until it is just beginning to turn golden. Add the chopped tomatoes and cumin, and season well. Reduce the heat to low and cook the relish for 30–35 minutes or until it becomes thick and pulpy.

2 Meanwhile, make the quesadillas. Sprinkle a tortilla with 40 g (1/3 cup) of the grated cheese, leaving a 1 cm (1/2 inch) border around the edge. Scatter 1 1/2 teaspoons of the Jalapeño chillies over the cheese and put another tortilla on top, pressing it down. Repeat the process with the remaining tortillas, cheese and Jalapeños until you have eight quesadillas.

3 Cook the chipolatas in a large frying pan over low heat, turning them occasionally, for 10–12 minutes or until they are cooked through. When the chipolatas are nearly ready, start cooking the quesadillas on a chargrill pan (griddle) for 1–2 minutes on each side, or until the cheese has melted. You may need to do this in batches, so make sure you keep them warm as you go.

4 Cut each quesadilla into quarters and serve them with the tomato relish and chipolatas, garnished with the sprigs of coriander.

blue cheese
and onion flan

PREP TIME: 40 MINUTES +
    40 MINUTES REFRIGERATION
COOKING TIME: 1 HOUR 40 MINUTES
SERVES 8

2 tablespoons olive oil
1 kg (2 lb 4 oz) red onions, thinly sliced
1 teaspoon soft brown sugar
185 g (1 1/2 cups) plain (all-purpose) flour
100 g (3 1/2 oz) cold butter, cubed
185 ml (3/4 cup) cream
3 eggs
100 g (3 1/2 oz) blue cheese, crumbled
1 teaspoon chopped thyme leaves

NUTRITION PER SERVE: Fat 38.5 g; Carbohydrate 26 g;
Protein 20 g; Dietary Fibre 3 g; Cholesterol 438 mg;
2205 kJ (525 Cal)

1 Heat the oil in a heavy-based frying pan over low heat. Cook the onion and sugar, stirring, for 45 minutes, or until the onion is caramelized.

2 Sift the flour into a bowl. Rub in the butter with your fingertips until the mixture resembles fine breadcrumbs. Make a well in the centre and add 3–4 tablespoons cold water. Mix with a flat-bladed knife, using a cutting action until the mixture gathers in beads. Gently press together and lift onto a lightly floured surface. Shape into a ball, wrap in plastic wrap and chill for 30 minutes.

3 Preheat the oven to 180°C (350°F/ Gas 4). Lightly grease a 23 cm (9 inch) loose-based flan tin. Roll out the pastry on a floured surface, and invert over the tin. Press in with a small ball of pastry, trim and chill for 10 minutes. Line the pastry with baking paper and fill with baking beads. Bake the case on a tray for 10 minutes. Remove the beads and paper, and bake for 10 minutes, or until pale gold and dry.

4 Cool, then spread the onion over the pastry base. Whisk the cream, eggs, cheese, thyme and some freshly ground black pepper together, then pour over the onion and bake for 35 minutes, or until firm.

coconut pancakes with bananas and syrup

PREP TIME: 20 MINUTES
COOKING TIME: 45 MINUTES
SERVES 4

150 g (5^1/$_2$ oz) palm sugar, roughly
    chopped, or soft brown sugar
2 tablespoons lime juice
125 g (1 cup) plain (all-purpose) flour
45 g (^{1}/$_4$ cup) rice flour
125 g (^{1}/$_2$ cup) caster (superfine) sugar
45 g (^{1}/$_2$ cup) desiccated coconut
500 ml (2 cups) coconut milk
2 eggs, lightly beaten
4 bananas, thickly sliced on the diagonal
2 tablespoons dark brown sugar
50 g (1^3/$_4$ oz) butter, plus 20 g (1 oz) extra
30 g (^{1}/$_2$ cup) shredded coconut, toasted
1 lime, cut into wedges

NUTRITION PER SERVE: Fat 53.5 g; Carbohydrate 131 g;
Protein 13.5 g; Dietary Fibre 9 g; Cholesterol 132 mg;
4340 kJ (1035 Cal)

1 Put the palm sugar in a small, heavy-based saucepan with 125 ml (^{1}/$_2$ cup) water and stir it over low heat for 5 minutes, or until the sugar has dissolved. Increase the heat to medium and let it simmer, without stirring, for 15 minutes, or until the liquid becomes a thick, sticky syrup. Stir in the lime juice and keep the syrup warm.

2 Sift the flours into a bowl, add the caster sugar and coconut, and mix. Make a well in the centre and pour in the combined coconut milk and egg, beating until smooth.

3 Toss the bananas in the dark brown sugar and add them to a frying pan over low heat, dotting each piece with butter. Cook the banana, turning the pieces occasionally, for 4–5 minutes, or until it begins to soften and brown. Remove from the pan and keep warm.

4 Melt a little of the extra butter in the pan and pour in 3 tablespoons of the batter, using the back of a spoon to spread it out to a 15 cm (6 inch) circle. Cook the pancake for 2–3 minutes, or until the underside is golden, then turn it over and cook the other side for another minute. As each pancake is cooked, transfer it to a plate and cover it with a tea towel to keep it warm. Add more butter as necessary and keep going until all of the batter has been used and you have eight pancakes.

5 Fold each pancake into quarters and put two on each serving plate. Top them with banana, drizzle each with a little palm sugar syrup, sprinkle with the coconut and serve with lime wedges.

apple and berry crumble muffins

PREP TIME: 15 MINUTES
COOKING TIME: 25 MINUTES
MAKES 12

155 g (1 1/4 cups) self-raising flour
150 g (1 cup) wholemeal self-raising flour
1/4 teaspoon ground cinnamon
pinch of ground cloves
115 g (1/2 cup) soft brown sugar
185 ml (3/4 cup) milk
2 eggs
125 g (4 1/2 oz) unsalted butter, melted and cooled
2 Granny Smith apples, peeled, cored and grated
155 g (1 cup) blueberries

Crumble

5 tablespoons plain (all-purpose) flour
55 g (1/4 cup) demerara sugar
35 g (1/3 cup) rolled oats
40 g (1 1/2 oz) unsalted butter, chopped

NUTRITION PER MUFFIN: Fat 13 g; Carbohydrate 40 g; Protein 4.5 g; Dietary Fibre 3 g; Cholesterol 37 mg; 1209 kJ (290 Cal)

1 Preheat the oven to 190°C (375°F/ Gas 5). Line twelve 125 ml (1/2 cup) muffin holes with muffin papers. Sift the flours, cinnamon and cloves into a large bowl, add the husks and stir in the sugar. Make a well in the centre.

2 Put the milk, eggs and butter in a jug, whisk and pour into the well. Fold gently until just combined—the batter should be lumpy. Gently fold in the fruit, then spoon the mixture into the muffin holes.

3 To make the crumble, put the flour, sugar and oats in a bowl. Rub the butter in with your fingertips until most of the lumps are gone. Sprinkle 2 teaspoons of the crumble over each muffin. Bake for 25 minutes, or until golden. Cool in the tin for 5 minutes, then transfer to a wire rack.

pistachio, yoghurt and cardamom cake

PREP TIME: 15 MINUTES
COOKING TIME: 55 MINUTES
SERVES 8

150 g (1 cup) unsalted pistachio nuts
$1/2$ teaspoon ground cardamom
150 g unsalted butter, chopped
185 g ($1^1/2$ cups) self-raising flour
310 g ($1^1/4$ cups) caster (superfine) sugar
3 eggs
125 g ($1/2$ cup) plain yoghurt
1 lime

NUTRITION PER SERVE: Fat 24 g; Carbohydrate 58 g; Protein 8 g; Dietary Fibre 2 g; Cholesterol 117.5 mg; 1990 kJ (475 Cal)

1 Preheat the oven to 180°C (350°F/ Gas 4). Grease a 20 cm (8 inch) round cake tin and line the base with baking paper. Put the pistachios and cardamom in a food processor and pulse until just chopped. Add the butter, flour and 185 g ($3/4$ cup) of the caster sugar and pulse for 20 seconds, or until crumbly. Add the combined eggs and yoghurt and pulse for 10 seconds, or until just combined.

2 Spoon into the tin and smooth the surface. Bake for 45–50 minutes, or until a skewer comes out clean when inserted into the centre of the cake.

3 Peel the zest off the lime with a vegetable peeler, then remove any white pith from the zest. Put the remaining caster sugar and 100 ml ($3^1/2$ fl oz) water in a small saucepan and stir over low heat until the sugar has dissolved. Bring to the boil, then add the lime zest and cook for 5 minutes. Strain and cool slightly. Pierce the cake with a few skewer holes and pour the hot syrup over the cooled cake.

strawberry cheesecake muffins with strawberry sauce

PREP TIME: 30 MINUTES
COOKING TIME: 15 MINUTES
SERVES 6

oil spray
250 g (1 punnet) strawberries, hulled
125 g (^{1}/$_2$ cup) caster (superfine) sugar
85 g (3 oz) light cream cheese
1 tablespoon strawberry liqueur
175 g (6 oz) plain (all-purpose) flour
1 tablespoon baking powder
1 tablespoon butter, melted
1 teaspoon finely grated orange zest
1 egg
125 ml (^{1}/$_2$ cup) skim milk
icing (confectioners') sugar, to dust

NUTRITION PER SERVE: Fat 5 g; Carbohydrate 47 g; Protein 7 g; Dietary Fibre 2 g; Cholesterol 41 mg; 1110 kJ (265 Cal)

1 Preheat the oven to 180°C (350°F/Gas 4) Lightly spray six 125 ml (^{1}/$_2$ cup) non-stick muffin holes with oil. Set aside six small strawberries.

2 Put half the sugar in a bowl with the cream cheese and mix together well. Put the remaining strawberries in a blender or food processor with the strawberry liqueur and remaining sugar, and blend until smooth. Strain through a fine sieve to remove the strawberry seeds.

3 Sift the flour and baking powder together into a large bowl and stir in the butter, orange zest and ^{1}/$_2$ teaspoon salt. In a separate bowl, beat the egg and milk together, then add to the dry ingredients and mix well until combined. Do not overmix.

4 Spoon half of the mixture into the muffin holes, then add a strawberry and a teaspoon of the cheese mixture. Top with the remaining muffin mixture and bake for 15 minutes, or until cooked and golden. Remove from the tins and cool slightly. Put a muffin on each serving plate, dust with icing sugar and serve drizzled with the strawberry sauce.

index